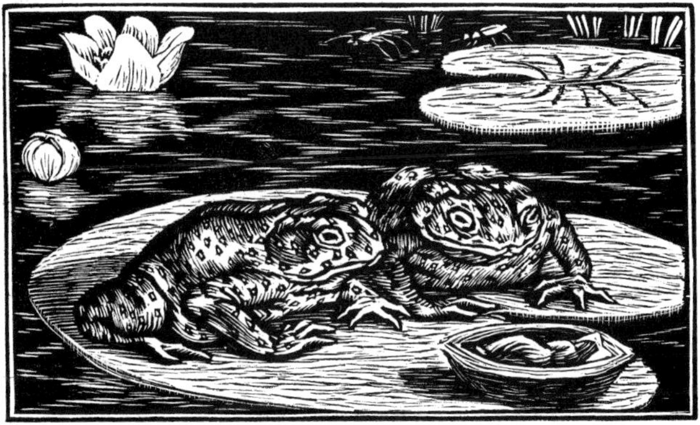

Thumbelina & the Toads[†]

[†]reduced

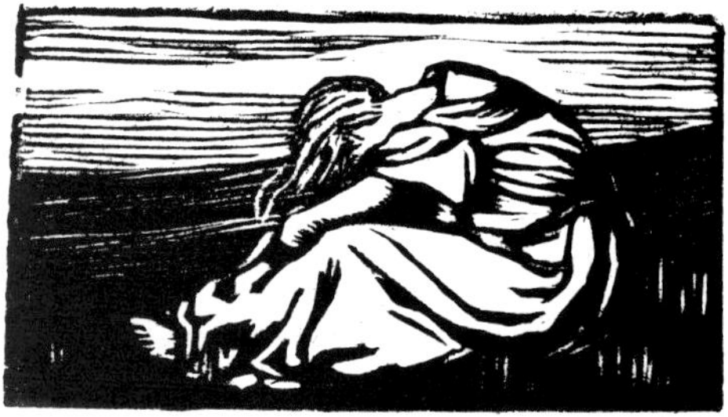

Despair

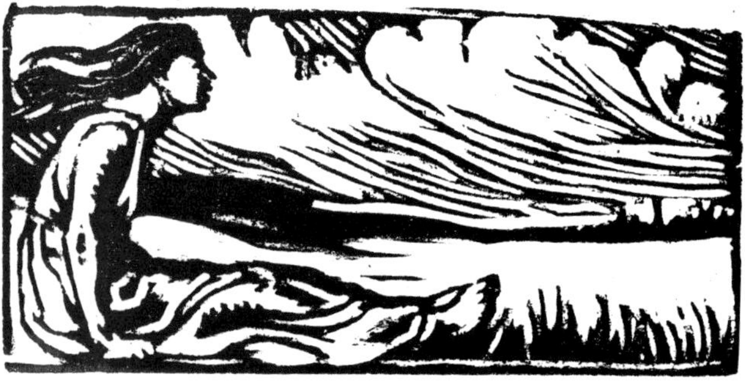

Windy Day

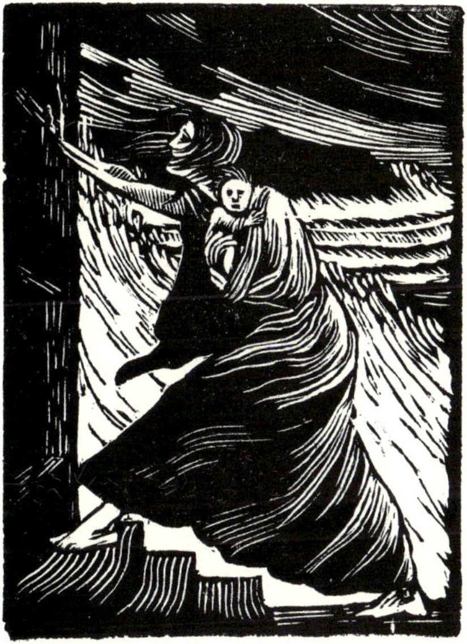

Annie of Rough Royal

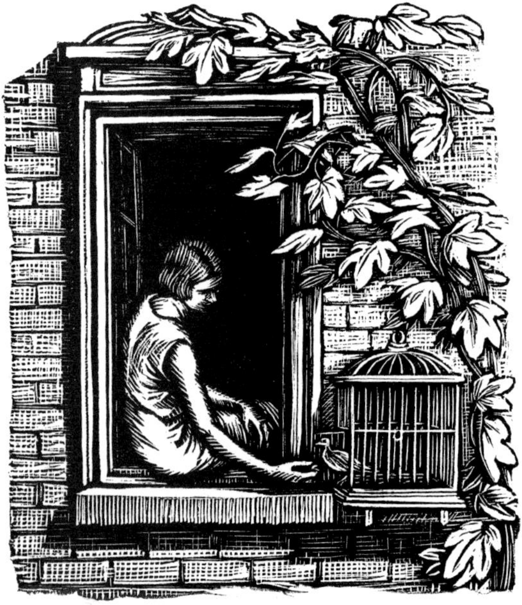

I had a dove

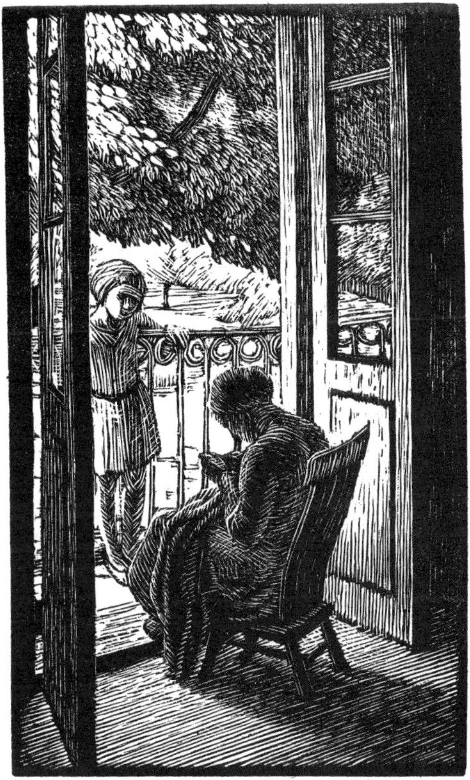

The Balcony

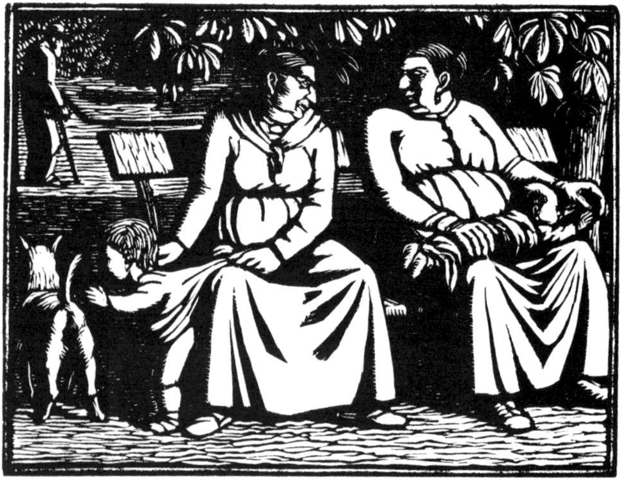

Scandal†

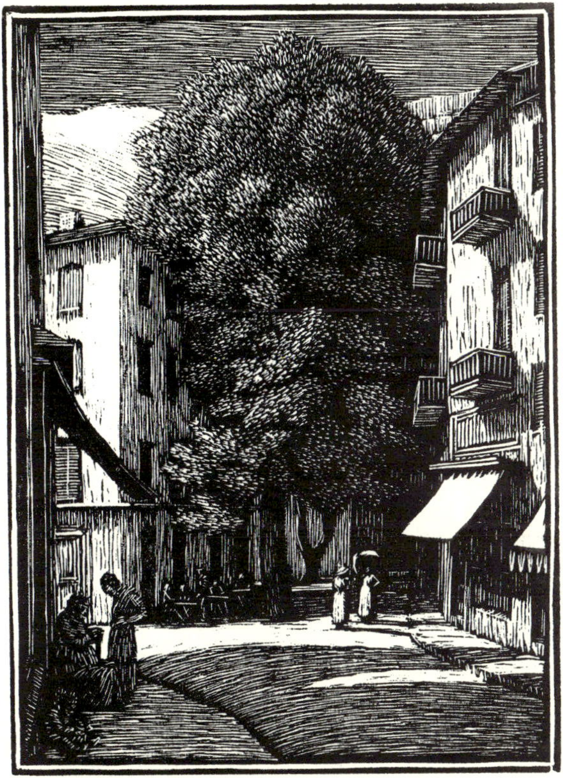

The Town in Summer

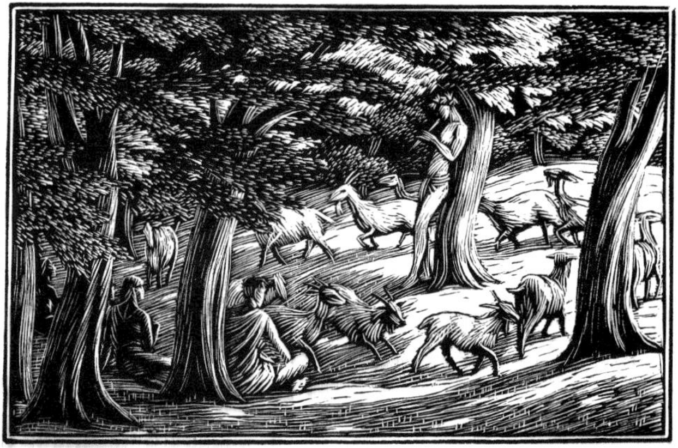

Daphnis Pipes to the Goats†

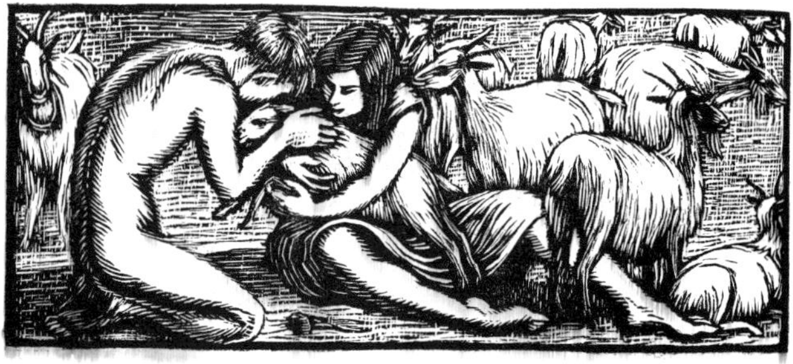

Daphnis Trims the Goats†

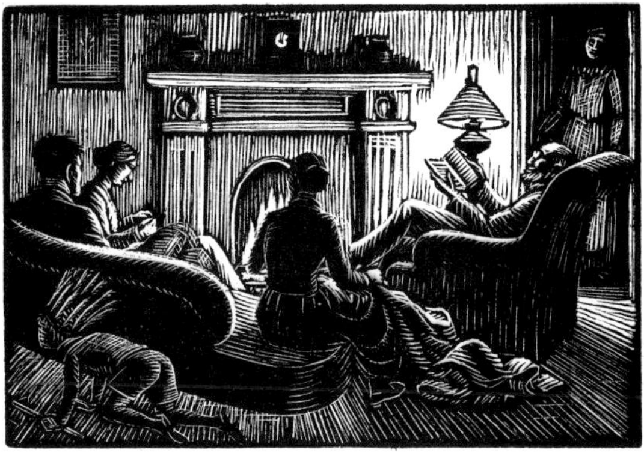

The Land of Storybooks

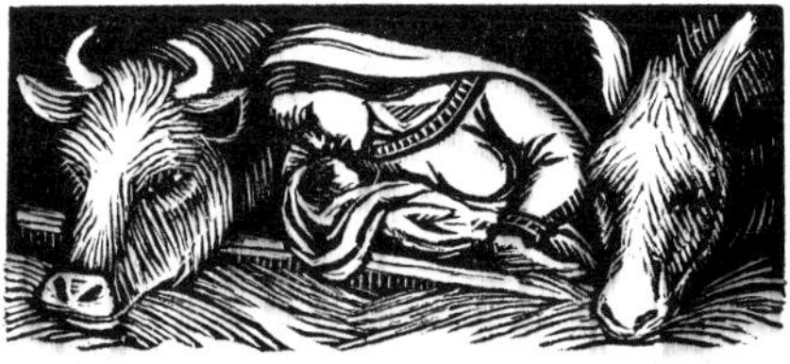

The Manger

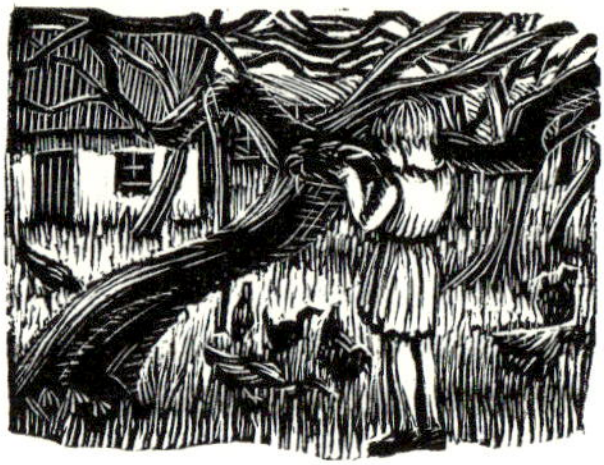

The Bird's Nest

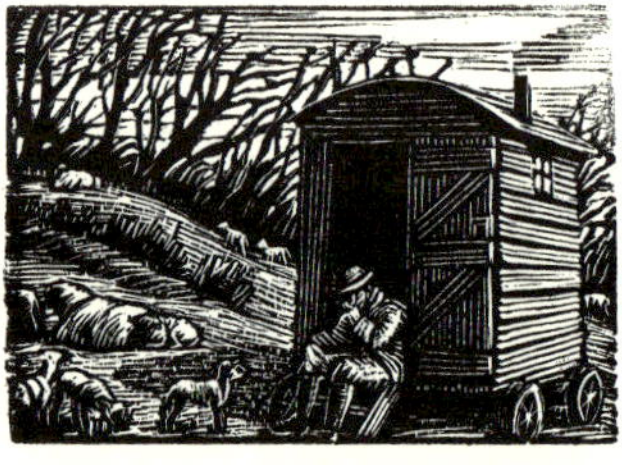

Shepherd

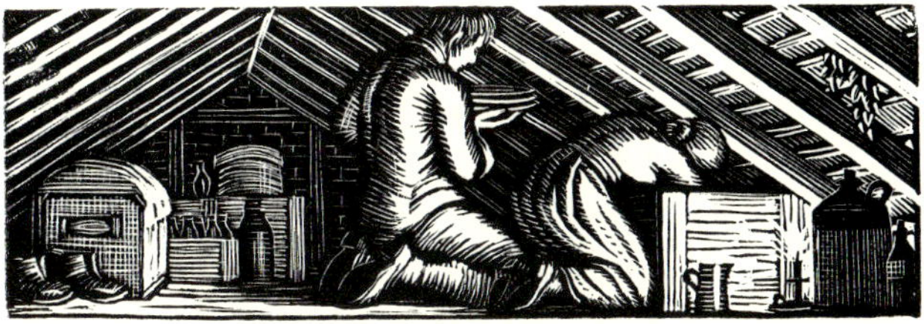

In the Loft

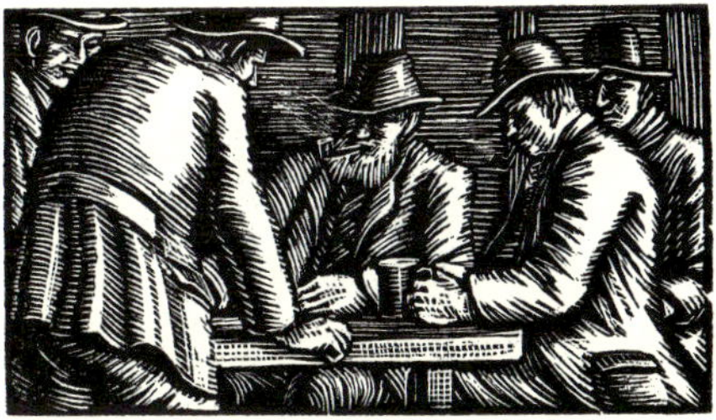

Country Conversation

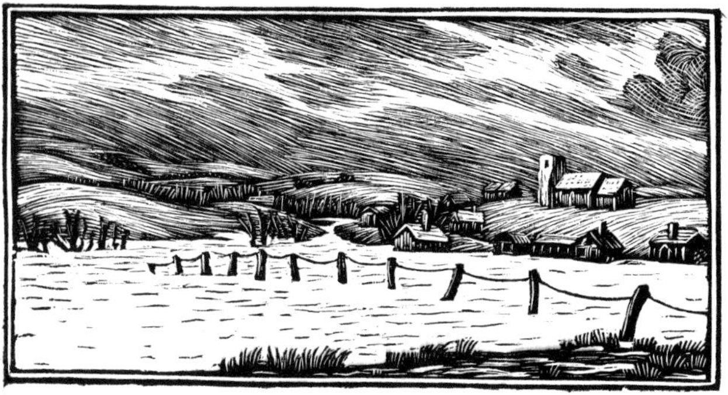

February†

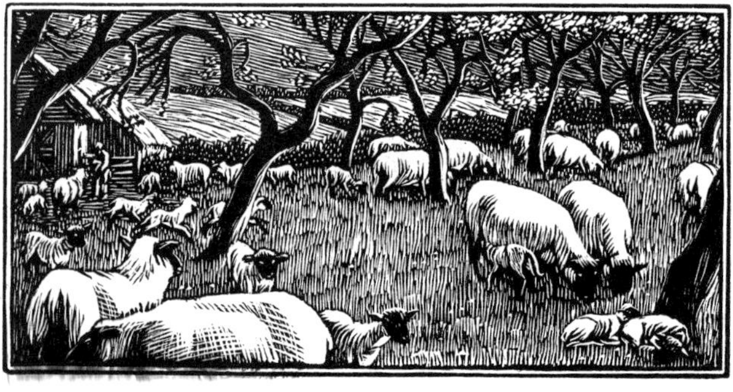

April†

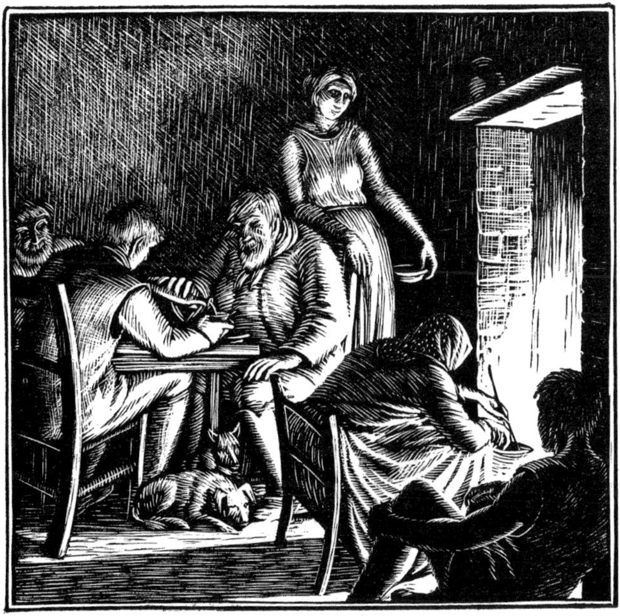

Winter Evening†

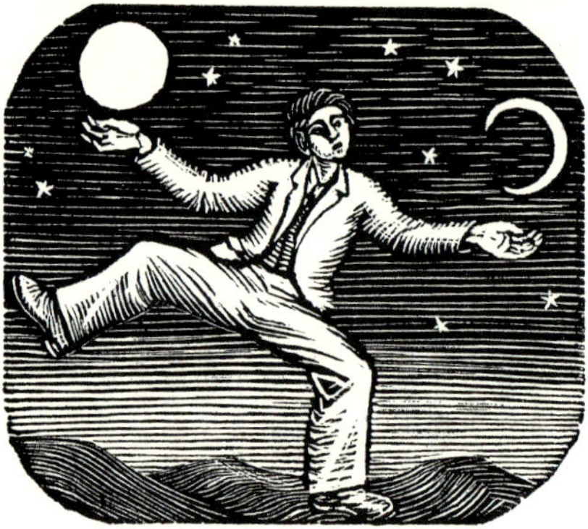

Fool's Song

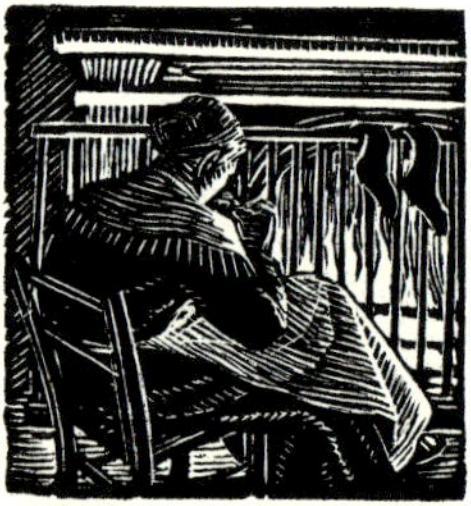

Nurse

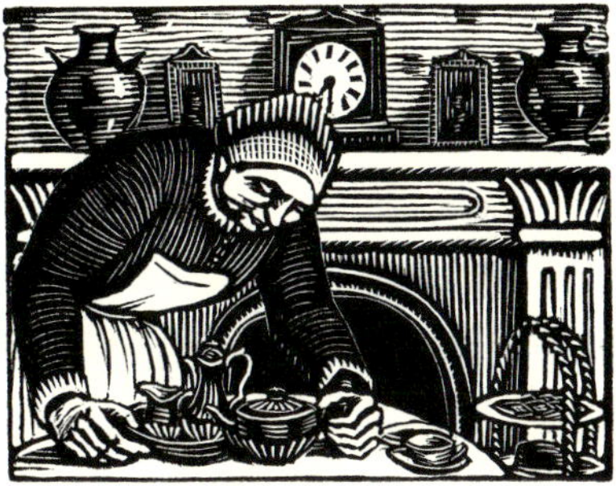

Louisa

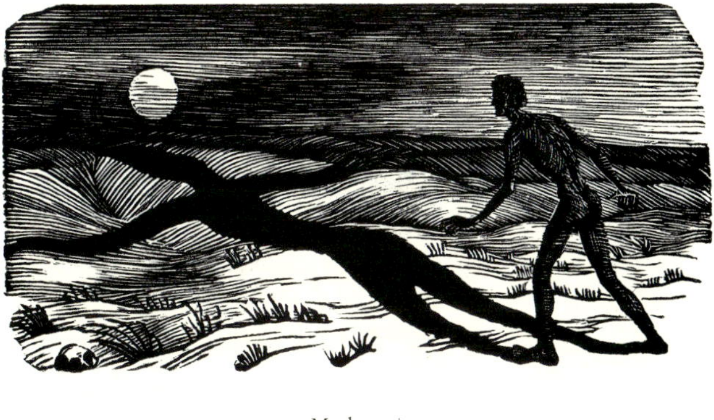

Madman[†]

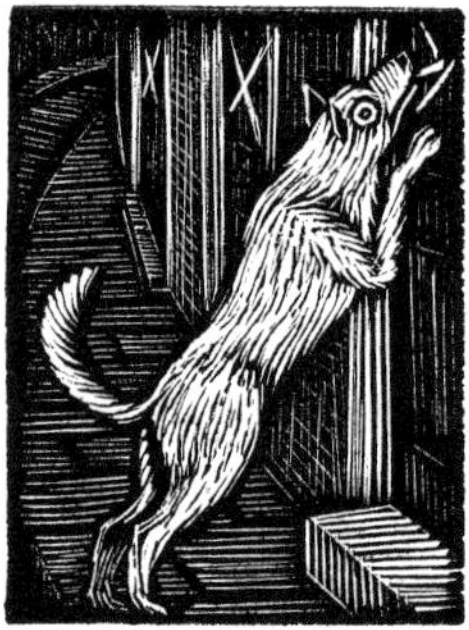

Dog Chalking Door

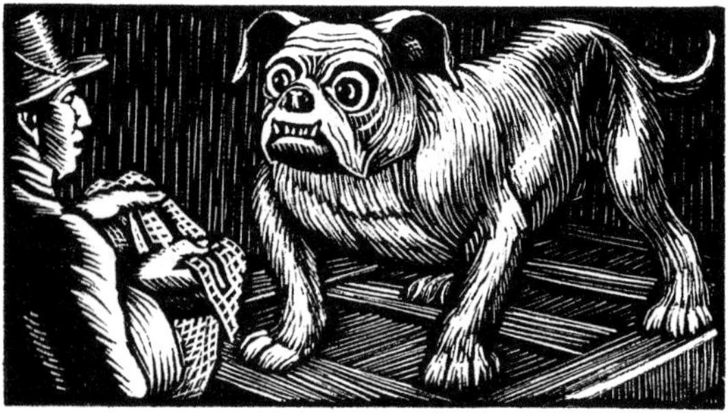

Second Dog